Original title:
The Blue Lagoon

Copyright © 2025 Creative Arts Management OÜ
All rights reserved.

Author: Christian Leclair
ISBN HARDBACK: 978-1-80581-510-5
ISBN PAPERBACK: 978-1-80581-037-7
ISBN EBOOK: 978-1-80581-510-5

Azure Reflections

In a pool so color bright,
Fish wear shades—they look just right!
Splashing water, laughter flies,
Goggle-eyed, we dodge the tries.

Rubber ducks float all around,
In this joy, we're tightly bound.
With a splash and silly dance,
We all grab our second chance.

Cerulean Dreams

In this hue, I lose my thoughts,
Building castles made of dots.
Why the sky is mad at me?
Oops! That wave was way too free!

Belly flops bring giggles loud,
I become a water shroud.
Why does sunscreen smell like cheese?
Could I swim with fluid ease?

Whispering Waters

Splish and splash, the fish are shy,
Turtles nod, and seagulls fly.
Frisbee flies then hits a tree,
Oops! Oh my! That's not for me!

As I dive for treasure missed,
All I found was moldy gist.
Laughing 'til the sun goes down,
Giggling like we'll never drown!

Hidden Oasis

In the shade of palm trees tall,
We sip on drinks—we spill them all!
Mermaids dance, but they're just friends,
Jerky snacks? Those are the trends!

Finding cool rocks, chips, and shells,
Hold your nose—it's funny smells!
Water fights can start the fun,
Who knew soaking could be pun?

Serenade of the Endless Blue

In waters deep, the fish do dance,
They wear bright hats, a fine romance.
A crab in shades, so cool and spry,
Winks at a starfish passing by.

A mermaid's laugh, it rings so sweet,
While turtles boast of fast retreats.
The sun slips down, and here we lay,
With seashells singing every day.

A dolphin's flip, a splashy show,
He steals the scene, don't you know?
Taste of salt and laughter loud,
We lounge around with joy, so proud.

The waves, they tickle our toes bright,
As we sip drinks from coconuts, light.
Here, every moment's a wacky spree,
In this endless blue, come laugh with me.

Whispering Echoes of the Sea

The ocean's whispers, secrets swell,
As seaweed giggles, oh so well.
A pelican wears a silly grin,
While waves keep slapping, teasing fin.

Fish play tag, in finny attire,
Wiggling about like they're on fire.
A clam sings tunes from deep within,
While crabs tap dance; oh, what a din!

With seashells' tales we fetch and find,
The silly shouts of sea combined.
The sun shines bright, our hearts ignite,
As water balloons take happy flight.

We're floating on a raft of cheer,
Making waves and tossing beer.
With every splash, our laughter flows,
In whispering echoes, joy just grows.

Where the Waters Hold Secrets

Under the waves, the fish confide,
In whispers low, they take a ride.
A turtle's laugh, so hard to catch,
He turtle-dances, what a stretch!

The depths conceal a party's call,
With mermaids giggling, trout and all.
A seahorse prances, wearing bling,
In secret corners, it's a swing.

A wave rolls in with prudent flair,
As sea creatures play truth or dare.
Octopus joins with jig and twist,
We hold our breath, they can't resist.

Beneath the surface, bubbles rise,
Of secrets shared and funny ties.
In this watery world, we can see,
Where laughter swims so wild and free.

Reflections in a Celestial Pool

Stars above in a sky so bright,
They wink at us, what a funny sight.
Reflections dance on water's face,
While fish do join in a cosmic race.

A wise old crab with glasses round,
Sips lemonade while we're unwound.
The sea cucumbers toss a party,
With jellyfish glowing, feeling hearty.

Seaweed sways like it's on a spree,
As pelicans croon in harmony.
With every wave, a joke takes flight,
In this celestial pool, pure delight!

Let's cheer to days without a care,
With laughter swirling everywhere.
In reflections, let's make a splash,
In this watery world, we'll always crash.

Calming Currents

On sunny shores, where laughter reigns,
The waves dance lightly, free of chains.
Crabs wear hats, the fish don ties,
A seagull jokes, under bright blue skies.

Beach balls bounce, in a game of fate,
While sunscreen slips, oh what a state!
Sandcastles tumble with a playful shove,
As jellyfish reel from the surf above.

Flip-flops flop, a chaotic sound,
As kids race on, round and round.
A starfish smiles, in the sand so grand,
Waving hello, like a friend so planned.

Turquoise Tranquility

In waters wide, so bright and clear,
A dolphin jokes, brings smiles and cheer.
Turtles in shades of peacock blue,
Dance with a wink, just for you.

Seashells whisper, with secrets sweet,
While crabs on their lunch break, pick up their feet.
A fish in a bowtie, curtsies with grace,
As laughter echoes in this playful space.

A beach bum's hat, too big for his head,
Turns into a sail, as he dreams in bed.
The sun plays peek-a-boo with the waves,
While every splash sends us into raves.

A Place Apart

In cozy nooks, where the sunbeam lingers,
Seagulls trade jokes with their silly singers.
Palm trees sway, with funky flair,
As flip-flops go flying through the salty air.

One surfboard thinks it's too cool to ride,
While turtles sneak snacks, eyes open wide.
Where the sand is warm, and the drink's a treat,
The bartender's jests can't be beat.

The picnic's a battle, a sandwich fight,
With crumbs that fly in a quirky sight.
But laughter erupts, and the world feels right,
In this sunny haven, so full of light.

Echoes of the Sea

The ocean's laughter rolls on the shore,
As fish tell tales of their underwater tour.
A pelican snores in a dream-like haze,
While starfish admire the sun's warm rays.

Waves that giggle, and break with flair,
Bring messages carried on the salty air.
A crab with a suitcase, ready to roam,
Waves goodbye to its soft sandy home.

Kids build forts, made of shells and sand,
While mermaids giggle, holding hands.
With jellybeans tossed and smiles that soar,
Together we laugh, forever wanting more.

Tranquility in Every Wave

Where fish wear tiny hats, they swim,
With bubbles saying hi, on a whim.
Seaweed dances with joy, so spry,
Shells gossip about the seagulls flying by.

A crab in a bowtie, quite the sight,
Has a little party, all night.
Turtles do the cha-cha, oh what fun,
Under the sun, they're never done.

Jellyfish juggle with grace, not a care,
While starfish cheer from their sandy chair.
The ocean laughs with a splash and a wink,
As dolphins meet up for a drink.

Seashells hold secrets of laughter and mirth,
In this watery realm, there's joy from birth.
Come join the fun in the sapphire embrace,
For in every wave, there's a smile on your face.

A Haven of Cerulean Calm

In a calm spot where mermaids breach,
They practice their puns, each a peach.
Crabs take selfies with sea urchins nearby,
While snappy fish sing wittily, oh my!

A pelican dives, missing the mark,
Plunges right in, making quite the arc.
Sea cucumbers laugh at the silly scene,
In this vibrant, watery carnival sheen.

Clams tell tales of the time they met,
A sandwich that tried to chat - you bet!
Waves roll in, tickling toes with glee,
Here, laughter flows like the salt in the sea.

Every splash brings cheers from the sand,
Where kids are busy, building castles grand.
In this funny nook of bright azure hue,
The ocean's jesters play just for you.

Waves of Whispering Serenity

Whispers ride the waves like boats,
Seahorses wear their finest coats.
A starfish's tale, quite the spread,
Of beach day pranks that left us all red.

Octopus paints with its eight long arms,
Murals of fish and their charming charms.
Crabs play poker, bluffing like pros,
While seagulls serve drinks and humor flows.

The tide rolls in with a giggle and dance,
Urchins have formed a merry romance.
Ocean's comedians crack up the crowd,
While shells echo laughter, joyful and loud.

Waves frolic and tumble, a merry affair,
In this sea's embrace, find laughter to share.
So swim in the humor, surf on the grin,
For joy in the deep is where you begin.

Azure Horizons Unveiled

Under a sky so silky and bright,
Venture where jellybeans take flight.
Ocean spray brings giggles all around,
As dolphins wear shades, they leap from the ground.

A flotilla of fish wear bow ties galore,
Popping in bubbles, they dance on the shore.
Seabirds trade jokes with the swell of the sea,
And laughter erupts like waves crashing free.

A guppy tells tales of the mainland bazaar,
Of pickles and jellybeans, the best by far.
Octopuses perform, their tricks a delight,
While crabs throw confetti, spreading joy in flight.

In this azure world, where smiles take wing,
Every wave carries laughter, joy's little fling.
So dive into joy, let your heart float away,
For in this bright ocean, it's always a play.

Requiem for Lost Shores

Once I sought a sandy throne,
But found only jellyfish — oh, what a groan!
As I dug my toes deep in the sand,
A crab pinched my toe like a little band.

Flip-flops flew in salty gust,
I held my drink, it spilled — a must!
Waves would laugh and tease my hat,
I chased it down, like a furry cat.

Sunburnt nose, I wore with pride,
In shades too big, I tried to hide.
With every splash, a squeal of glee,
And awkward dances, just for me.

But with each tide that sweeps away,
My dreams of sun and fun must sway.
I bid adieu to all despair,
As seagulls steal my fries — how unfair!

The Sunlit Embrace

Beneath a sun that's far too bright,
I wear a smile, though not quite right.
Suntan lotion, oh what a chore,
Slippery hands, I drop it more and more.

I flopped on floats, quite round and grand,
Like a beach ball misjudged by the sand.
With children giggle-splashing near,
I can't escape this childish cheer.

A wave comes crashing, takes my chair,
Soaked and shocked, I gasp for air!
Up on my feet, ready to dash,
But tripped on flippers — what a crash!

Still, laughter bubbles in each splash,
I greet the sun with exuberant flash.
In waves of fun, this jester reigns,
While sunscreen glides like slippery chains.

Untamed Waters of Tranquility

In crystal depths where mermaids play,
I tried to swim and lost my way.
I splashed and sank like a heavy rock,
Then came up laughing, just to gawk.

A seal swam by, with a funny face,
He winked at me — I joined his race.
With fins that flopped and splashes wide,
We twisted, turned, in ocean's tide.

The giggles intertwined with waves,
As fish swam by with their little braves.
I'd dance with dolphins, what a sight,
But they just swam off, without a bite.

Alas, my treasure, just some sand,
Yet joy and laughter fill this land.
With tangled hair and fishy smells,
I leave the sea with silly tales.

Dreaming Under Cerulean Skies

With azure dreams of cotton clouds,
I lounged about, no worries allowed.
Then birds flew past, with honks and screeches,
I followed them — oh, how life teaches!

A gentle breeze tickled my nose,
I waved at strangers — heaven knows!
They waved back, and I felt so bold,
Turning pink with stories told.

Ice cream drips trail down my hand,
The sun now scorched my pale, pale sand.
With sprinkles sliding, oh what a mess,
A seagull swooped, and I must confess!

I laughed so hard I lost all grace,
In my sandy dress, I lost the race.
Under cerulean skies so wide,
Who cares! I'm here, enjoying the ride.

Vast Cerulean Calm

In a sea so bright and blue,
I lost my shoe, oh what to do!
Fish are laughing, making waves,
While I search for my footwear graves.

Sun is shining, birds all sing,
But where's my hat? It's gone, the thing!
Splashed my friend, they yelled with glee,
I just wanted a sip of tea!

Turtles lurking, what a sight,
Trying to swim but lost the fight.
Caught a sunburn, bright as a flame,
But still I dance, what a wild game!

At dusk we feast on silly snacks,
With beach ball fights and crazy hacks.
Laughter echoes, filters on,
Our funny tales, they linger on.

Embraced by Waves

Waves are giving me a smack,
Salty water, what a whack!
Jumped right in, with all my clothes,
Now my outfit swims, goodness knows!

Seagulls squawk like they've lost their minds,
Diving down; oh, such unkind finds!
Floating here, I take a break,
But the tide says, 'No time to make!'

My friends are building castles tall,
Till a wave comes and makes them fall.
Sandy hair and silly grins,
We laugh till the setting sun begins.

Endless fun and splashy cheer,
I'll take this vibe all through the year!
With giggles loud, we'll jump and sway,
Embraced by waves, we dance all day.

Waters of Rejuvenation

In waters that sparkle and shine,
I sip coconut, feeling fine.
But oops! I dropped my fruity drink,
Now fish swim by, I really stink!

The sun is burning, oh what a tease,
I tried to float, but oh dear knees!
Water's cool, I take a dive,
Gasping loudly, I'm still alive!

A clam just whispered, 'What's the fuss?'
I answered back, 'It's all about us!'
Bubbles rising, laughter bubbles too,
In this paradise, just me and you.

With silliness all around,
My troubles vanish, they can't be found.
In depths so vibrant, we seek delight,
Waters of joy, we stay all night.

Serene Shallows

In shallow pools, we splash and play,
Collecting shells to show and sway.
Hermit crabs are judging me,
For my dance moves, oh can't they see?

Twirling 'round with arms like wings,
Pretending I'm a fish who sings.
Seashells clatter, what a sound,
Echoes of laughter all around.

Bubbles popping, a cheerful tune,
Dancing shadows, morning to noon.
Caught a wave, but lost my hat,
Oh where's it gone? I'm in a spat!

Lunchtime comes, we feast with glee,
Sandy sandwiches, what a spree!
With giggles and mischief, we splash some more,
In these serene shallows, who could ask for more?

Liquid Dreams of Blue

In a splash of azure glee,
Fish wear shades, sipping tea.
Mermaids giggle, flip and flop,
While the dolphins prance, never stop.

Sandcastles stand, oh so grand,
Built by the crabs with a steady hand.
Seagulls squawk, a comedic rap,
As tourists stumble, take a nap.

Floating on floats, all a drift,
Sunscreen slathers, such a gift.
A beach ball bounces, takes a dive,
Who knew this place was so alive?

Sunsets paint the sky with cheer,
As we toast to laughter and a beer.
In this realm of silly dreams,
Life is just bursting at the seams.

Horizon's Gentle Embrace

Waves roll in with a squeaky laugh,
As jellyfish dance and take a bath.
A squirrel steals a snack, oh dear,
While we sip drinks and munch on cheer.

A diver's flip lands on a seal,
Who swats him back with a fishy meal.
A sandman lounges, sunbaked and free,
A crab plays tag, oh such a spree!

The clouds gather for a fluffy race,
While children try to keep up pace.
Each splash and giggle breaks the calm,
We're all wrapped up in this balm.

As night falls, lanterns swing,
Our laughter rises, what joy they bring.
With dancing feet and hearts so bold,
This horizon's laughter never gets old.

Tranquil Excursions in Azure

Boats bob on the glassy waves,
As sea turtles roll like little knaves.
Chasing the sun with angler's bait,
We giggle loud at our own fate.

A picnic is set with quirky treats,
Ants march in like tiny fleets.
Lemonade spills – oh what a scene!
Frog hops in, joins our cuisine!

Laughter echoes, a vibrant tune,
As a crab plays checkers beneath the moon.
With kites that fly and spirits high,
Adventure unfolds as the day goes by.

Stars twinkle down, with a wink and a grin,
As we share our dreams, where do we begin?
In these tranquil woods of azure delight,
Our hearts dance and feel light.

Ephemeral Moments in Cerulean Light

A beach ball's thump makes a ruckus loud,
As sunbeams wink from behind a cloud.
Though the tan lines are a funny sight,
Our spirits soar with sheer delight.

The sunbird whistles a quirky song,
While turtles cheer and dance along.
A surfer stumbles, oh what a save,
His splash is met with a dolphin wave!

Pineapple floats, help us unwind,
As crabs parade, their dance so blind.
Glasses raised, we toast the day,
In this silly land, let troubles stray.

As dusk wraps us in its tender fold,
We cherish moments, brave and bold.
For in this light of a cheerful scroll,
We find laughter to fill the soul.

Bliss Beneath the Aqua Folds

In waters bright, we splash about,
With rubber ducks, we laugh and shout.
A seagull stole my snack today,
I chased it off—what a wild fray!

Beneath the sun, we twist and twirl,
Our beach ball flies, a bright white pearl.
A crab joined in the game of chase,
But only crabs can win that race!

My friend got stuck—oh what a sight,
In floats so big, she took off like a kite.
We giggled hard, then splashed her back,
Our laughter echoed, oh what a crack!

The tide rolled in, it took our toys,
We shrieked with fun, those squeaky joys.
So here we stay, just being fools,
In aquamarine, we make our rules!

Driftwood Dreams Amongst the Waves

A stick I found, I claimed it fast,
In my grand ship, we sail at last.
But oh dear! The sea is mean,
It tossed me off—my ship was seen!

With driftwood crowns, we rule the shore,
Each crab a knight, we hark the roar.
Seashells sing, they hold our tales,
While dolphins dance and join our gales!

We gather round, our kingdom grows,
With sandy thrones and shells for bows.
The tide comes up—our fortele slowly,
But look! A wave is creeping—oh so lowly!

Who knew the sea was such a tease?
It gives us fun, then takes with ease.
We'll laugh and cry, and laugh some more,
In our woodsy dreams by the ocean floor!

Poetic Pursuit of the Blue

Oh, for the sea, our silly muse,
The daring waves wear crazy shoes.
A fish swam by, with quite the grin,
It winked at me, a cheeky fin!

We built a castle, oh so grand,
With jelly parts—an odd demand!
A crab sat high, with royal flair,
But when it pinched, I had to swear!

The tide came in, our castle fell,
We shrieked and laughed, oh what a spell!
A starfish waved, it joined the fun,
Reigning together, puddles run!

So let's embrace this silly fate,
To dance with sea, to laugh, await.
For in the blue, we find delight,
A world of joy, both day and night!

The Enigma of Wandering Waters

In mystery deep, the waters churn,
With every wave, we take our turn.
A rubber whale did take a dive,
And nearly made my friend arrive!

With silly games, we have our cheer,
A floaty race, let's make it clear.
My sunhat flew, it flew so high,
And danced upon the clouds of sky!

We chased a fish that seemed to mock,
While tripping over bits of rock.
It slipped away, oh what a tease,
Soon joined the tides in jovial breeze!

So here we splash, through giggles bright,
In wandering waters, pure delight.
As secrets hide in endless blue,
We chase our dreams, with laughter too!

Beyond the Blue Embrace

In a place where mermaids sing,
And fish wear hats that make them bling,
I splashed through waves with glee so bright,
Chasing crabs into the night.

Seagulls steal my sandwich cheat,
While dolphins dance with joyful feet,
Sunburnt noses and sandy toes,
What a life! Who really knows?

Bright umbrellas shade my drink,
With a tiny straw, I start to sink,
Flip-flops flying everywhere,
Laughing now, who can compare?

The sun is hot, the tide's a prank,
I lost my towel, that's a rank,
But in these waves, I found my muse,
Silly fun, you cannot lose!

Nautical Nirvana Awaiting

In a cove where laughter flows,
A walrus plays a game of prose,
I tripped on flip-flops, what a sight,
As seaweed tickles my delight.

Jellyfish bounce like jolly clowns,
And crabs parade in tiny gowns,
I tried to dance with all my grace,
But fell right into my own face.

My drink umbrella floats away,
As I chase it in pure dismay,
The tide decides to play its game,
And I'm the one who's feeling shame.

Yet through it all, I laugh aloud,
While seagulls form a silly crowd,
For in this place of azure hues,
I find my joy, I cannot lose!

Radiant Waters of Nostalgia

Beneath the sun, we dive and splash,
With floating noodles in a clash,
A turtle steals my snack with ease,
As I flounder and beg, "Please!"

My sunscreen's on a fishing boat,
The waves now sing a funny note,
A sea star's caught in my hair,
What a mess for joy to share!

The anchor's lost, I can't believe,
"Just relax," my friend deceives,
We float along like silly fools,
Making waves while breaking rules.

So here's a toast to sandy sights,
With laughter echoing in the nights,
With radiant waters all around,
It's where my silly joy is found!

Dips in Azure Serenity

On a raft that wobbles 'round,
I sip my drink; it makes a sound,
A seagull lands right on my hat,
    What a crafty little brat!

With every splash, the laughter roars,
The tide is playing knock on doors,
My friends all cheer, "Come take a dip!"
As I fumble with my flip-flop grip.

The sun is shining, oh so bright,
While fish show off their belly flight,
    Octopuses offer goofy waves,
  In this spot, we're all quite brave!

So join the fun, don't miss the boat,
We'll ride the waves and shake afloat,
  In this paradise of pure delight,
We'll laugh and splash from day to night!

Symphony of the Sea's Embrace

In a cove where the seagulls sing,
The silly fish wear a bling.
Jellyfish dance in a wobbly line,
While crabs do the cha-cha, looking just fine.

Driftwood floats like a lost canoe,
While the sun slides down, turning pinkish blue.
A starfish claims its sandy throne,
Waving at tourists, never alone.

The waves tickle toes on the shore,
And clam shells giggle, wanting more.
With seashells as hats, the crabs like to prance,
Making the beach their goofy dance.

Underneath the sky's pastel hue,
Sandy feet try to catch a seagull or two.
Nature's laughter in the salty air,
In this funny realm, we all just share.

Nautical Sanctuary

A little boat with a silly grin,
Bobs and weaves like it's trying to win.
Octopus chefs cook up a storm,
While dolphins join in, making it warm.

With flip-flops flying, what a sight!
Sandcastles stand, but not for long, right?
Our beach ball bounces with joy and glee,
While the tide plays tag with a giggly spree.

Seaweed wigs in a fashion show,
Sea turtles laugh, what a funny flow.
When sea foam laughs and insists it's cream,
We're here to swim, dance and dream!

As the sun winks, the waves just smile,
Splashing around, we stay a while.
In our nautical sanctuary, jokes unfurl,
As the whole ocean becomes our world.

Cerulean Bliss Awaits

Beneath the sky so brilliantly blue,
The fish plan pranks; oh, what a crew!
A crab with sunglasses poses in style,
While a mermaid winks with a cheeky smile.

The seabeds dance with colors so bright,
And sea cucumbers giggle at night.
Turtles wear ties for the grand ball,
While sea urchins roll, having a ball!

Waves bring whispers of secrets untold,
As sea stars twinkle like treasures of gold.
With every splash comes a ticklish cheer,
In cerulean bliss, laughter is near.

So join the fun in this ocean spree,
Where even the barnacles dance with glee.
In this place of joy under the sun's rays,
Remember, fun is the only phrase!

Waves of Memory

As the surf comes in with a playful grin,
Seagulls giggle, they're up to a win.
With flip-flops flapping, the race is on,
And sandy pies made, just for fun!

The tide playfully teases our toes,
While clams and shrimp share silly woes.
A dolphin flips and takes a bow,
While sandcastles topple, oh, what a wow!

With laughter rolling in every wave,
We chase the sunset, oh, how we crave!
In a world of bliss where joy is the key,
Waves of memory, come dance with me!

So as this ocean story unfolds,
Let humor reign; let the laughter hold.
With salty air and sun that beams,
We weave our fun in ocean dreams.

Elysian Waters of Reverie

In a pool of laughter, we dive,
With seagulls squawking, we thrive.
Swimwear mishaps, oh what a sight,
Sunscreen debates under the light.

Splashing about, the kids run wild,
While parents just grin, oh so riled.
Sand castles crumble, oh what a fail,
Yet giggles bounce like a boat with a sail.

Ice cream drips down a sunburned chin,
"Just one more scoop!" they insist with a grin.
The tide comes in, washing feet all clean,
In this watery world, we're all just teens.

As sunset hues flicker, we sing,
Of mermaid dreams and legendary bling.
With laughter and tales till it's time for sleep,
Of this paradise, we shall always keep.

A Lullaby in Shades of Aqua

In aqua dreams, I drift away,
Where dolphins dance and whales play.
Flip-flops flopping, as we roam,
In this watery land, we find our home.

A seagull swoops, steals our fries,
With a cheeky squawk, oh what a surprise!
Sand in our hair, laughter in the breeze,
This time together is sure to please.

Water pistols flying, laughter erupts,
While sunscreen battles make us abrupt.
A beach ball bounces, then takes a dive,
In this crazy world, we come alive.

As night falls soft, the stars convene,
With jellyfish glowing, a magical scene.
Under the moon, we dance and sway,
In aqua lullabies, forever we'll stay.

Reflections of an Endless Ocean

Behold the waves, they twist and turn,
Each splash a giggle, our hearts they churn.
Sandy toes and a sunburned nose,
This ocean of joy, it surely flows.

As seagulls squawk, they join our song,
With mixed-up words, we sing along.
A hat takes flight, oh how it twirls,
In this goofy realm, our laughter unfurls.

Mismatched swimsuits, style oh-so bold,
With tales of triumph, and others retold.
Shells we collect, some shiny, some not,
In this ocean of dreams, we find our spot.

As the tide rolls in, we're swept away,
With playful antics, we spend our day.
Reflections sparkle, in moonlit motion,
In this vast expanse, we're lost in devotion.

Exhale Among the Tides

In the morning light, we make our splash,
With laughter and giggles, oh what a bash.
Buckets and shovels, our tools of delight,
Building dreams in the sand, oh so right.

The waves, they whisper secrets to the shore,
As we chase the foam and shout for more.
A crab scuttles by, shares quite a glance,
In this land of fun, we twirl and prance.

The sun begins to dip, painting the sky,
"Who wants more ice cream?" we loudly cry.
With dripping cones and sticky delight,
Our evenings sparkle, under stars so bright.

So let's embrace this life by the sea,
Where every wave's a dance, wild and free.
Exhale the worries, in laughter we glide,
With hearts open wide, we'll enjoy the tide.

Lagoon's Lullaby

Splashing fish dance with glee,
While crabs wear hats, oh can't you see?
Penguins waltz in a funky way,
As sea turtles groove, please stay and play.

Frogs croak tunes that tickle the air,
Seagulls squawk gossip, quite the affair.
Driftwood floats like it's on parade,
While colorful shells join the masquerade.

Palm trees sway with a chuckling sound,
As sandcastles topple, tumbling down.
A dolphin juggles in a blue haze,
While giggles echo across sandy bays.

So come join the fun, don't be shy,
Splash in the surf, let out a huge cry!
Wave to the sunset, it paints us bright,
In this silly spot, everything feels right.

Twilight Ripples

As dusk falls gently on the shore,
Mermaids argue over fashion galore.
With starfish strutting on tiny feet,
And sea cucumbers buzzing to the beat.

Moonlight sparkles on glistening waves,
Where wise old octopuses tell tales from caves.
Clams giggle softly, hiding their pearls,
While jellyfish shimmer, twirling and swirls.

The night creeps in, lanterns ignite,
With shrimp in disco lights, what a sight!
Tiny crabs breakdance, legs askew,
These silly creatures just might fly too!

So raise your glass to this quirky crew,
And toast to the fun, the mischief they brew.
In twilight's embrace, come laugh and play,
For every heartbeat here's a goofy ballet.

Heavenly Waters

Up in the clouds, the mermaids splash,
Wearing sunglasses, having a blast.
Coconuts giggle, journey astray,
While sunburned seagulls plot their next play.

Clouds drift by in a fluffy parade,
As dolphins prance, unafraid.
With flip-flops dancing on toes so tan,
And turtles planning their next game plan.

Bubbles float like balloons in the breeze,
Everyone's laughing beneath swaying trees.
A picnic of snacks, sandwiches galore,
Oh, what a joy, who could ask for more?

So dive in deep, let your worries fly,
In these heavenly waters, we can touch the sky.
Jokes weave like currents, laughter will flow,
In this joyful haven, let your spirit glow.

Beneath a Sapphire Sky

Under the sun, where the silliness reigns,
Laughter like waves, it never wanes.
Floats on the water, a quirky parade,
With rubber ducks in a grand charade.

Kites dance high, soaring around,
As seaweed wigs flop on the ground.
Giant sandcastles tickle our toes,
While crabs play tag, nobody knows.

The horizon giggles, kissing the sea,
As we splash around, so wild and free.
Funny fish jokes make us snort and cheer,
In this crazy bluescape, we banish all fear.

So gather your pals for a bubbly delight,
With sun-drenched fun till the fall of night.
Each splash a punchline, each wave a jest,
In this whimsical world, we're truly blessed.

Oceans of Rediscovery

In waters bright, we paddle with glee,
A splash here, a laugh there, wild as can be.
Flip-flops and sun hats, a colorful crew,
Chasing bubble-blowing fish, oh, what a view!

Cantankerous crabs dance on the sand,
While seagulls practice their personal brand.
The sun stole my drink, can't find it now,
A tropical mystery, oh where, oh how!

A boat drifts by, its passengers scream,
We wave and laugh; they are part of the dream.
With ice cream cones melting at lightning speed,
The ocean's a canvas of laughter we need!

So here's to the tides, the surf, and the fun,
Where silly moments shine just like the sun.
In every splash lies a memory we make,
A wacky sea tale, for goodness' sake!

Horizon of Stillness

A hammock sways in the soft, warm air,
With towels piled high, they're everywhere!
Seaside siestas take center stage,
While sandcastles rise like a golden age.

The old guy's snoring, mouth wide, oh dear,
A wake-up call from a seagull near!
We dare each other for a daring dive,
Then cannonball into splashy high five!

As the sun sets low, the sky's a delight,
Dancing shadows tell tales of the night.
But watch your toes, there's a crab with a grudge,
In this silly paradise, we'll never budge!

Laughter spills like waves on the shore,
In this tranquil zone, we always want more.
With each giggle, it's magic unfurled,
A moment of joy shared, across the world!

Wandering Through Blue Enchantment

Underneath the sky, so vast and blue,
We journey together, just me and you.
Splashing through shallows, the world feels bright,
Trading silly looks, it feels so right!

A dolphin does flips, we cheer with delight,
He's the water's own star, so fast, so light!
Flip-flop fiascos leave us in stitches,
As we discover the ocean's many riches.

A treasure map sketched in crayon and sand,
Leads to a stranger's unclaimed ice cream brand.
We dip our toes in, then giggle and squeal,
Because everything's funny with just a meal!

Dive under the waves, forget all your strife,
In this whimsical world, laughter's the life.
With bubbles of joy floating all around,
Wandering through blue, magic can be found!

The Depths of Serenity

In crystal waters, we find our peace,
Where ducks wear sunglasses, and troubles cease.
A beach ball rolls off, chased by a pup,
Oh, the joy that unfolds as we give chase up!

Tanned toes wiggle in the soft, warm sun,
While goofy beach antics have only begun.
Sunblock fights and laughter in the air,
Making memories with all to spare!

A curious crab in a top hat and tie,
Waves us hello as he scurries by.
"Good day, my friends!" he seems to say loud,
"Join in the fun, come dance on this cloud!"

As the waves draw near, let's soak in this glow,
With every splash, more laughter to sow.
In the depths of this joy, let worries float free,
For here in this moment, it's only you and me!

Island of Dreams

On an isle where coconuts sway,
Tourists dance the day away.
Seagulls laugh as they pass by,
Wishing they could try a pie.

Sunburned noses turn to red,
While the crabs chase up ahead.
A flip-flop flies, oh what a sight!
Even the fish swim with delight.

Sandy feet and salty air,
Frolic like you haven't a care.
Ice cream drips, a funny treat,
Chasing cones with quickened feet!

At night we gather round a fire,
Sharing tales that never tire.
Laughter echoes, the stars gleam bright,
As we roast marshmallows tonight!

Dappled Light on Water

Sunshine dapples, making waves,
Jellyfish dance, oh how they crave!
Kicking surf and splashes free,
Send the laughter up a tree.

Bikini tops are flying high,
Oh dear, look, a seagull's spy!
It snatches snacks with speedy glee,
While everyone shouts, 'Oh, not me!'

Umbrellas tilted, who can tell?
Sunscreen battles, oh, what a sell!
The sand is hot, the drinks are cold,
The tales of epic beach days told.

As sun sets low, the fire's bright,
Guitars strum through the gentle night.
The sand feels cozy, the mood's just right,
Tell me again why we took that flight?

Azure Embrace

A hammock sways with gentle glee,
Cracking jokes with the palm tree.
Splashing water, oh what a mess,
Finding shells is anyone's guess!

Floating like a cork at sea,
A lobster yells, 'Come play with me!'
Tanning spots that look like art,
Red and white, now that's a start!

Rainbows shimmer in the foam,
As we pretend this is our home.
The fish roll their eyes with a grin,
And we just can't stop this chagrin!

Then sunset draws with hues so bright,
We sip our drinks, oh what a sight!
With laughter echoing through sheer bliss,
This azure life is one we miss!

Serene Waters Whisper

Whispers flow in the ocean breeze,
Pineapple drinks that aim to please.
Waves crash softly, a gentle hug,
While we search for a charming bug!

Snorkels on, we dive right deep,
Silly fish swim, not a peep.
Lost in bubbles, oh what fun,
Giggling loudly, under the sun!

Sunset paints the sky with grace,
As we apply our last sunscreen base.
Why did Bob wear two left shoes?
Now that's a tale we can't refuse!

As night drapes down with silver stars,
The tweak of joy comes from our cars.
Driving home, we hum a tune,
Dreaming of the next trip soon!

Luminous Hues

In a world painted with silly shades,
Where fish wear hats and mermaids fade,
A beach ball rolls with a goofy bounce,
While sunburned folks dance like they pounce.

The waves giggle as they chase the sand,
With seagulls squawking a humorous band,
A crab on crutches hobbles by,
Singing a ditty about the sky.

In the twilight, laughter swirls around,
As clumsy turtles flip without a sound,
Everyone's smiling, despite the heat,
With ice cream dribbles and sticky feet.

So come and join this vibrant scene,
Where joy swims in hues of bright green,
Forget your worries, play in the sun,
A day in this paradise is all in good fun.

Cradled in Blue

In a cradle of waters, laughs abound,
Where jellyfish giggle, twirling around,
A buoy bobs like a cheeky friend,
Whispering secrets that seem to bend.

With flip-flops flying, each stroll is a show,
Sandy toes squish, oh how they grow!
Waves crashing hard like a slippery slide,
Skimming the surface, it's a wild ride.

Beach chairs wobble, a sight to behold,
As sunscreen fights against the sun's hold,
Everyone's merriment rises to the top,
With laughter echoing, it simply won't stop.

In the embrace of this joy-filled tide,
Leave all your troubles safely aside,
For here in the blue, fun is a must,
In a lively haven of colorful trust.

Solitude by the Shore

A lone seagull struts with flair,
Wearing a scarf, he doesn't care,
Shells whisper jokes as they tumble by,
While seaweed sways, an impromptu tie.

Sandy castles built to tip over,
As kids in hats play their game of poker,
Ice cream cones melt, a sticky mess,
As laughter bursts forth, no need to stress.

A dog on a raft floats far too high,
Chasing after waves as they pass by,
While beachgoers cheer for his brave feat,
Taking a plunge, he lands on his feet.

In this solitude, humor holds sway,
As the sun dips down to end the day,
So gather your friends, make some noise,
For life's too short not to enjoy joys!

Quiet Respite

Where the moonlight dances on silver waves,
And crickets chirp like melodious knaves,
Under the stars, they gather, no fear,
Sharing funny drinks that bring hearty cheer.

With tiki torches flickering bright,
A parrot squawks jokes in the still of night,
Blankets sprawled out, all cozy and neat,
S'mores in hand, it's a tasty treat.

Giggles erupt as stories unfold,
Of epic fails, and antics so bold,
Sandcastles collapsing in fits of glee,
In this holiday haven, we're wild and free.

So here's to the laughter, the fun, the light,
In this tranquil spot, where magic feels right,
A quiet respite, filled with delight,
Where silly moments shine ever so bright.

Tidal Serenade of Calm

Waves splash like giggling friends,
Seashells dance as laughter blends,
Crabs in tuxedos scuttle around,
Nature's jesters in a watery town.

Fishes flash their silly grins,
Doing laps like tiny twins,
A seagull drops a sandwich with flair,
Ocean's humor floats in the air.

The sun winks down, a cheeky tease,
As kids build castles with salty breeze,
Buckets tip, and laughter spills,
Joy bubbles up like fizzy drinks' thrills.

So let the tides tune the song,
In this splashy haven, we all belong,
With giddy waves and a salty breeze,
Let's float on fun, if you please!

Azure Dreams on Gentle Shores

Footprints in sand, a comical trace,
Where seagulls strut, the kings of the place,
Belly flops and splashes galore,
The ocean's a stage, always wanting more.

Beach balls bounce with cheerful grace,
While children giggle, a playful race,
Sun-kissed noses, funny tan lines,
Chasing the waves like silly designs.

Sandy sandwiches, sticky and sweet,
An ice cream cone? Now that's a treat!
Seashell souvenirs in pockets reside,
Reminders of laughter enjoyed by the tide.

So let's dive in, with joy we soar,
On these gentle shores, who could ask for more?
With waves that tickle and suns that shine,
Let's make today a silly sunshine!

Oasis of Liquid Sky

In this watery world, we find our play,
Floating like marshmallows, we drift away,
Rubber ducks sail with noble pride,
A flotilla of fun on the ocean wide.

Snorkelers wave, looking quite silly,
As otters glide by with their playful frilly,
Each splash of water a giggly cheer,
Echoing laughter, it's perfectly clear.

Sunsets paint skies in hues so bright,
While dolphins leap in a comical flight,
Their playful antics make us all grin,
In this liquid sky, let the fun begin!

So grab your floaties, and let's take a spin,
In this vibrant oasis, the laughter won't thin,
With splashes and gasps, we'll dance on the tide,
A whimsical escape, with joy as our guide!

Hidden Under Waves of Blue

Beneath the ripple, secrets hide,
A party of fish in a shimmering ride,
Octopuses juggle with fins and a wink,
While sea cucumbers just like to sink.

Starfish lounge in a lazy array,
While turtles play tag, in their own way,
A coral clown dresses up in bright hues,
In this wacky world, it's all fun and blues.

The rhythm of waves, like laughter's echo,
Tales of the tide, where giggles do flow,
Sand in our toes, with a wink and a grin,
Explorations begin, let the fun times spin!

So dive right in, don't mind the splash,
Under these waves, we'll make a splash,
With smiles wide and hearts so free,
Join the ocean's dance, come swim with me!

Submerged in Silken Blue

In waters deep, we splash about,
With giggles loud, our joys shout.
Rubber ducks float, a silly sight,
Sunblock splattered, what a delight!

Mermaids giggle, tails askew,
Unruly waves, they join our crew.
We dive for treasures, a shoe, a sock,
Where is the treasure map? Oh, what a shock!

Sunscreen's scent, a fragrant blend,
Gooey hands, our hearts do bend.
Belly flops and cannonballs,
In this blue charm, fun never stalls!

With noodle floats, we paddle along,
Singing off-key, our goofy song.
In this blue oasis, laughter reigns,
We'll take on the world's silliest claims!

Pools of Serenity

In quiet pools, we dip our toes,
With rubber rings, our laughter flows.
The sun beats down, we bake like bread,
Who stole my shade? The sneaky head!

A splash, a trip, oh what a fall,
My friends shout out, ``Now that's a ball!``
We waddle by, such graceful sights,
With water wings, we ignite our flights.

The ducks in rows, a parade of fun,
Join our shenanigans under the sun.
With laughs and splashes, we create our art,
These silly moments warm my heart.

"Floaties here, who's got my snack?"
In pools of joy, no way we lack.
With every giggle, the stress just fades,
United in chaos, our friendship trades!

The Call of Turquoise Depths

Oh, in the depths of bubbly bliss,
We tumble down, with wild misses.
Flip-flops flying, a stylish dance,
How did I wear two pairs by chance?

The turquoise calls, a playful tease,
As we dodge splashes, with utmost ease.
An octopus waves, or so it seems,
Are those his tentacles or just our dreams?

Underwater selfies, bubbles galore,
We capture moments worth shouting for.
Every goofy grin, our smiles so wide,
In the turquoise embrace, we take pride!

As sunbeams tickle, we chase the light,
In this realm of laughter, everything's right.
So here's to the fun, the shenanigans bright,
In these depths of laughter, our hearts take flight!

Dance of the Gentle Tides

The gentle waves, they sway and spin,
With boogie moves, we dive right in.
Splashing around, a competitive race,
I swear that wave just contrived to chase!

Our beach ball bounces, a laugh machine,
With every hit, we wreak chaos unseen.
Who's got my flip-flop? A quest today,
In this wobble of fun, we simply play.

The sands are hot, our footprints blend,
With water fights, our laughter transcends.
The tide rolls in with a playful cheer,
Let the dance of the tides erase our fear.

So here we swirl, through sun-kissed rays,
On waves of joy, we'll spend our days.
With every ripple, we sing our song,
In this zany tide, we all belong!

Embrace of the Tide

In the sun, we snack on fries,
Seagulls swoop and squawk, oh my!
A splash here, a splash there,
Water's cold, but I don't care.

Bubbles rise like party balloons,
We dance with the waves, sing to the tunes,
My floatie's shaped like a giant shoe,
Best idea? Yeah, I thought so too!

Laughter rings out, we're wild and free,
Splash fight? Oh yes! Come get me!
Life's too short to sit and mope,
We're riding high on the wave of hope.

The sun sets low, with a wink and a grin,
With sandy toes, we all dive in,
Tonight we feast on marshmallow s'mores,
In our embrace, we'll always want more.

Sapphire Serenity

Tons of snacks on the beach we've spread,
While jellyfish dance just ahead,
I scream, 'Is that a wave or a whale?'
Turns out it's Bob, trying to sail!

With laughs and giggles, we're splashing around,
Bob's floatie bursts—a comical sound,
He paddles like a frantic fish,
Just one look, and I can't resist.

Sun hats askew and sunscreen in eyes,
We're mermaids and pirates under blue skies,
With each goofy slip, our spirits soar,
Life's a carnival and we're the main shore.

As the sun dips low, we wave goodbye,
But not before we give it a try—
A dive off the dock, we're flying high,
"Cannonball!" declares me, with a gleeful cry.

Enchanted Eden

A beach party? Count me in!
With weird-shaped fruits and a big grin,
We mingle like waves, fun is a must,
Sandy toes and snacks; it's a cosmic trust.

A crab strolls by, posed like a star,
I ask, "Where's the beach party? Near or far?"
He clicks his claws, does a little jig,
Turns out crabs dance really big!

With sunburned noses, we sing out loud,
Dancing like seaweed in a wobbly crowd,
Each twirl and spin brings giggles anew,
Even the fish dance in shades of blue.

As stars pop out and the night draws near,
We toast with coconuts, spread the cheer,
Our island's alive with laughter and play,
In this enchanted place, we'll forever stay.

Lapping Blue Embrace

Waves waltz gently, a crisp ballet,
Tickling our toes as we laugh and play,
"Can you catch me?" I shout with glee,
But the ocean just giggles and splashes me!

With inflatable turtles, we float with grace,
Bob's holding on tight, what a funny face,
He slips off smooth and into the spree,
"I'm back!" he shouts, "Was it deep?" Not me!

Grabbing snacks as we run off the sand,
I trip over my towel; isn't life grand?
With guffaws that echo above the surf,
Above all, it's joy that we all are worth.

Even the sunset wears a goofy grin,
As friends unite, let the antics begin,
With a blast of color and giggles in the air,
We float in this laughter, no worries, no care.

Mysteries Beneath the Surface

In waters deep, fish wear a frown,
They're flipping about like they're swimmin' in town.
A crab with shades shows off his dance,
While starfish gossip of their last romance.

A octopus sits on a throne made of kelp,
Holding court with the dolphins and a very wise whelp.
They chuckle and joke about sailors who swim,
And wonder aloud how life's gotten so dim.

The turtles race with a cheer and a puff,
One claims he's faster, although that's just tough!
They all gather 'round to play a silly game,
Where seaweed is prize for the biggest name.

As bubbles rise up and the currents swirl,
The clownfish giggle, giving tails a twirl.
In this world below, laughter leads every day,
Beneath the blue waves, they bubble and play.

Tranquil Blue Voyage

Sailing the sea on a boat made of dreams,
With fish that wear hats and floaty moonbeams.
A parrot on deck chirps a tune oh-so-cheerful,
While a playful dolphin thinks he's a real steal.

The captain, a seagull, squawks with delight,
He insists that the stars can navigate right.
But each time he charts, we just end up adrift,
As jellyfish giggle, giving us a good lift.

With snacks made of seaweed and a sandwich of sand,
We munch and we slurp, it's all quite unplanned!
The waves provide laughter as splashes go wide,
And soon we're all soaked, it's a wild, crazy ride.

So here's to the seas, with their odd little quirks,
Where laughter and friendship are all that it lurks.
With each funny wave and each silly squawk,
This tranquil journey is the best kind of talk.

Aquatic Canvas of Serenity

A painter's dream lives where the water is bright,
With colors so wild, they leap at the sight.
A fish with a palette splashes colors so bold,
While sea frogs serenade stories once told.

The corals are canvases combined and arrayed,
With a swirl of a brush, they're painted in jade.
Anemones dance with the rhythm of tides,
While the lobsters critique from their cozy hides.

The shrimp form a band, with maracas and beats,
As grouper critics nod while tapping their feats.
There's laughter and music in a splashy refrain,
As bubbles of joy rise up, glistening plain.

Each stroke tells a tale, each wave marks a thought,
In this whimsical world, we're all happily caught.
So let's dive in deep, where the joy's a sensation,
In this aquatic creation, the pure celebration.

Celestial Waters

Under the stars where the moon shines so bright,
Little fish wish on wishes for dreams taking flight.
With a wink and a wiggle, they dance in delight,
While crabs put on shows in the shimmer of night.

The plankton twinkle like diamonds afloat,
While squids write poems on seaweed with hope.
An oyster chuckles at the humor of life,
Telling tales of the sea that carry no strife.

As mermaids dive under the seas made of glass,
They tickle the turtles and wink as they pass.
"Join us!" they call, "For a swim in the dream,
Where laughter is plenty and fun reigns supreme!"

So revel in ripples where the stars start to gleam,
In waters celestial, we float and we beam.
With giggles and splashes, the night flies away,
In the sparkle of water, we happily play.

Hidden Dreams

In the depths where the seaweed sways to and fro,
Little fishes whisper of things they could know.
A squid with a funny hat gives directions each day,
While snails slide around in a leisurely way.

There's treasure untold just beneath the blue hues,
Like a ship made of candy with a crew full of booze.
The lobsters hold court, wearing crowns made of vinyl,
As octopuses juggle for a giggle, quite final.

A sea cucumber dreams of becoming a star,
While the shrimp and the crabs cheer him on from afar.
And each passing wave brings a new silly scheme,
As dolphins agree, "Let's live out our dream!"

So dive into magic of depths unconfined,
Where laughter and fish tales are meticulously entwined.
For in this wild water, joy swims all around,
And happiness sprouts every time they're unbound.

Reflections of Tranquil Depths

In a pool where ducks play hide and seek,
A fish tried to sing, but it smelled quite weak.
Sunbathers giggled with glee and delight,
As sunscreen battled the seagulls in flight.

With splashes and laughs, the water did splash,
A flip-flop went flying, oh what a crash!
The sun wore a grin, blazing down with cheer,
While our beach ball decided to drift far from here.

The sand clung to toes, causing quite the fuss,
We rolled in embarrassment, oh what a plus!
With drinks in hand, we toasted to fun,
While the crab danced away, thinking he'd won.

As twilight approached, the laughter grew more,
With rumors of mermaids and treasures in store.
But the only real catch, as we soon discovered,
Were chips and dip, and the sun slowly covered.

Sapphire Secrets Beneath

Beneath the waves, where secrets reside,
The clumsy fish danced with the tide.
An octopus juggling, what a wild sight,
While turtles played tag, oh what a delight!

Coral reefs chuckled, in colors so bright,
As starfish formed parties, deep into night.
Anemones swayed, like they knew the tune,
While the seaweed swirled, like a green polka moon.

A crab wore a bowtie, looking quite posh,
But tripped on his pinchers, oh goodness, what a wash!
With laughter erupting from shells near the sand,
The whole ocean joined in, making waves by hand.

As we dipped our toes, our day felt complete,
With laughter and joy, and tasty fish treats.
So here's to the wonders, both funny and bright,
Hidden beneath waves, where giggles take flight.

Dreaming in Azure Hues

In a dream where the sky and water entwine,
Jellyfish performed, each one a headline!
Bubbles floated up, like balloons in the air,
While dolphins spun tales, no worries or care.

With every splash, a laugh would erupt,
As a clam cracked a joke, the crowd got hiccuped.
Seagulls joined in, with their squawky refrain,
As we all laughed loudly, forgetting the strain.

The sandcastles built were a sight to behold,
With moats made of laughter, and stories retold.
As the sun painted skies in rich golden light,
We danced with the waves, what a glorious sight!

So here's to adventures, both silly and sweet,
In this whimsical world, where laughter is neat.
With friends by our side, and smiles all around,
We dream in blue hues, where joy can be found.

Echoes of a Crystal Cove

In a cove where giggles bounce off the shore,
We chased after waves, shouting 'more, more!'
A sandpiper strutted, a true fashionista,
While crabs offered tips, 'wear shells, not a fiesta!'

The tide pulled back, revealing tales untold,
With treasures of shells and stories bold.
A mermaid flipped her tail, made a huge splash,
While all of us cheered, in a jubilant dash.

Beneath the bright sun, our laughter rang clear,
As we built giant castles, without any fear.
Old seagulls sat perched, judging our craft,
While we took selfies, embracing each laugh.

As the day melted down into pastel skies,
We packed up our memories, basked in the highs.
With promises made for adventures anew,
In our crystal cove dreams, forever we'd stew.

www.ingramcontent.com/pod-product-compliance
Lightning Source LLC
Chambersburg PA
CBHW072131070526
44585CB00016B/1625